Burning the midnight oil

Jason Sellers

Presentation by *BookLeaf Publishing*

Web: www.bookleafpub.com

E-mail: info@bookleafpub.com

ISBN: 978-93-95755-88-7

First edition 2022

DEDICATION

To Sheena for always believing in me and my grandma who showed me the way

The one

We go through life finding love and finding our
own way through the world,
Never knowing if we will ever find that one
special boy or girl.
We date and they seem a good fit until we find
out they aren't the one after a couple years
We never know when or who the right person
will be and we will shed many tears
Then all of a sudden without warning someone
comes in your life and you just know that they
are the one,
You start to feel different emotions or feelings
toward this person

Sunshine Queen

Her face is like a ray of sunshine, she speaks no ill will to anyone only words of kind.

When she enters a room it fills with light when she smiles, her voice is that of an angel that you can hear from miles.

When you cast your eyes on her she will be the most beautiful woman you have ever seen, she is unlike any I have ever met and when you do be sure to bow to the sunshine queen.

Madly in Love

When I look at you from across the room my
heart flutters and you take my breathe away,

I feel in the moment jno one else matters just
you and me I want this moment to last and do I
pray.

I am madly in love with this woman who
captured my heart and made me feel alive once
more,

I don't feel pressured or forced to do things I do
them willingly unlike my past before.

I am madly in love with this woman that cares
how I feel and makes me be a better man,

I want to walk in the woods and explore things I
never seen, dance with you in the rain I want to
love you the best I can.

I am madly in love with this woman who will
never feel alone or afraid for I will never let
harm come her way,

She is the happiness I have been looking for the
love I have craved, and the one I would never
betray.

Twin Flames

As I search for the woman that will fill my heart
she is searching for me to feed her soul, I keep
searching through the years not knowing when
she will appear and make me whole.

Just as I search for her, she continues to seek out
me and find her twin flame her one true
soulmate, she faces pain and regret but still she
knows I am still out there and still I wait.

Then out of the blue when we both don't expect
it two halves searching for the other crosses
paths, our eyes lock onto each other and the heat
from our flames burns brighter as if by
command.

So here we are twin flames growing in love just
as it was meant to be, showing the world how
life is to be lived just you and me.

Never to late

I lay here with a cigarette in my hand
My mind is a prison of unwanted thoughts and
how my years were spent.

As the cigarette burns slowly down to the end
of of the butt,
I continue down my path of despair and
depression now I am stuck in this rut.

My phone never rings no one knows how far I
haven fallen now is when I need a friend,
But I hear no one asking how I am or asking me
to hang out I know this is the end.

You see posts on social media never wait till it's
to late to tell someone you love them,
But I guess they will have to sleep never
knowing how this became so grim

I take one last drag of my cigarette before I
crush the life out of it and to seal my fate,
All I need is one person to tell me they are there
for me before it's to late.

I check my phone one last time and still not one
text or call with tears in my eyes I put the gun to
my head,
I say a small prayer for my family and friends
before I fill myself with lead.

I steady my hand choke back tears as I get ready
to do this horrible thing,
As I cock the hammer back and begin to pull the
trigger before I hear click I hear a ring.

Grandma

You have been there with me from the start
I hold you close to my heart.
I sat with you as we listened to gospel songs
You taught me right from wrong.
We have been close through the years
You always told me with God we have nothing
to fear.
I have tried to live the Christian way
But over the years I have strayed.
I know we are not promised tomorrow
And the world is full of sorrow.
But thanks to you teaching me about the devil
and his lies
You helped me find God and opened my eyes.

Hell

I wake up from a mental daze,
I can't see through this smokey haze.
The smoke burns my throat and lungs,
It's hotter than a million Sun's.
I try to walk but it feels my feet are made of
lead,
As I continue to walk I see a body with out a
head.
I fall to my knees and begin to scream,
I pray and hope this is all a dream.

As I walk through the valley of death,
I see something that takes my breath.
It's a lake of fire as far as the eye can see,
I can hear the screams of souls this is where I
don't want to be.
I have heard stories of this place it's hell for sure,
This is a place for evil beings not the pure.
I fall to my knees and pray to God above,
To take me out of here and show me His love.
I have lived my life and this is my fate,
But to you I say change your ways before it's to
late.

Freedom

I took my life for granted,
I took what I needed or wanted.
Had no guilt or any shame,
I was good at the game.
But it cost me my freedom.

I am shackled by my sin and in a cell,
surrounded by four walls this has to be hell.
I want to escape, I want to be free,
I scream THIS IS NOT FOR ME.
where is my freedom?

Seems I have been here for years,
my eyes are dry I have no tears.
I hear a click as the door swings open,
The light is bright is this my hope?
A voice tells me all is paid for,
I tremble afraid to go through the door.
as I walk through the door i got my...

FREEDOM!

Open Arms

I will come to you with open arms in your time
of need,
It doesn't matter your color, sex, or creed.
I will lift you up when you are weak or tired,
And welcome you home when your time on
earth has expired.
I will never leave you when you need me the
most,
Let your soul guide you to your heavenly host.

My church will greet you with open arms,
They will show you love and compassion.
They will be there if you feel lost or alone,
You won't feel like a stranger around them you
will belong.

I want you to greet people with open arms,
Never raise your hand out of anger or to cause
harm.
When a person comes to you that is hurting or in
pain,
Open your arms and tell them what they can
gain.

Never turn a blind eye or a deaf ear to those in
need,
Never waste food when you know someone it
could feed.
Teach them my message topics not hate,
And soon we all will meet at the pearly gate.

Lies

I will whisper ideas in your ear,
None of them good ones I fear.
I will tempt you each day of your life,
Like cutting school,stealing,or cheating on your wife.
I am the one who lies to you when I get the chance,
I am the one who will destroy your budding romance.
With your spouse,children, and God.

I am the one your bible warned you about,
The more you lie,cheat,or steal the harder I will be to
get out.
I am all around, you won't ever be rid of me,
Just ask your pastor, even with Jesus you'll never be
free.
I will bide my time,
Tell your soul is mine.

I will do what ever it takes to make you fail,
Then I will drag your soul to hell.
Just remember I am always looking out for you,
And never will judge the things you do.

Signed,
Satan

Numb

I feel so damn numb,
My thoughts are lies am I that dumb?
Why would anyone ever love me,
I am nothing more than a monster can't they see.
I show no love only hate, and I know death is
my fate.
I try to find one to love me for who I am, but
alas love seems lost damn.
My numbness has effected my heart, I feel it
tearing and breaking apart.
There is no stopping any of the pain, it seems
my emotions are locked in a chain.
Is there anyone that can set me free? All I can do
is wait and see.
I am at my breaking point, my life is going up in
smoke like a joint. I have suffered way to much,
my emotions have been like a crutch. I drank
half a bottle of whiskey now I feel loose, I will
say one more thing as I slip on the noose. Why

Reality

Everyone thinks that I am this happy go lucky
guy but that's just what I let them see,
I am actually an asshole, cheat, and always
depressed that's the real me.

If I had to say something nice about myself that
I actually like about me,
It's that no matter I am a loyal friend and would
help others in need that's how I will always be.

I don't care what people say or think about me
their opinion doesn't really matter,
As long as I stay true to myself I am sure I could
always do better.

My love

Make me ask your name
To perfect strangers
Make me question why our paths have crossed
Engage with me,
Whisper to me about who you are and convince
me to believe your existence.
Don't allow me to
Forget that you are a verb.
Your actions speak life,
Truth,
And hope.
Listen to all that I am and pray I show you more.
What is your name, love?

Once before

When even my dreams involve assisting you in
something beautiful, my heart remains unsure. I
don't aim for pain like I did once before.
I only crave acceptance , love, shared
daydreams, and hope for tomorrow.
Can we share this new energy?

Please.

Winter wonderland

Christmas time is here again listen to the holiday
cheer,
Couples hand in hand through a winter
wonderland.
See the Christmas tree and lights,
Shinging all through the night.
Children sledding in the snow,
And warming by the fires glow.
Looking out toward the winter wonderland.
Watch people's spirits lift,
As they open their Christmas gifts.
But let's not forget the special one,
Who was born on this day God's only son.
For he is the reason for Christmas,
Not for Santa or his lists but for one of God's
greatest gifts.

The last score

The last score... be it show time. Here, and together, just like the curtains before they start to slide.... Just apart like a waining tide. Pride? Was out the window pain and living in the foreboding minds eye for the seated spies... of the last score. There was a hole tore and set forth in the unwinding threadbare tapestry. Unveiling the facade... blink... a choppy breath inhaled violently and suspended... hand in hand intertwining fingers clinched... paused... still waiting... like a birth, something of a reborn entry. Lustfully yet listless... gathered for one more show........ Just, one. more. show.

Wake up

I have kept my tongue silent for to long,
America is slipping into more and more chaos or
am I wrong?
Have we turned a blind eye to 9/11?
Did we lose our faith in our lord in heaven?
The media shows us what they want us to see
Full of lies and half truths that most believe.
We have fell silent to scared to speak up for
what's right, Christians have been hated and
pushed so far down away from the light.

Wake up our country is slipping away soon it
will be to late, our freedom and constitution is
not up for debate. The constitution is "WE THE
PEOPLE" not WE THE GOVERNMENT,
while they get more powerful we get poorer and
can barely buy food,clothes or pay rent.
We have become a country of hard work and
earning what we worked for, to a country that
demands things for little or no work and expect
others to pay more. We give our children cell
phones, tablets or any kind of electronic device,
instead of playing tag,riding bikes or asking
their parents for advice.

We need to wake up as a country and protect our
freedom from those who seek to take them away.
We have a president who is willing to protect
our rights but there are others who tell us he is a
dictator or so they say.
We need to secure our southern border before we
are over ran by our enemies of the UNITED
STATES,
But there are people who say that is
unconstitutional and is wrong but those same
people are protected by walls and gates.
I feel America has turned its back on GODS
word and followed the world,
We have turned our backs on our children were
we can now legally kill babies both boy and girl.
As I write these words I hope and pray God will
touch your heart and bring this country back
together before we tear it apart.

Prison song

It all happened on a cold January night, when
the cops handcuffed me I was in a fright.
They told me all my rights and put me in the car,
as they talked to me I knew the station wasn't
far.
I tried to plead my case and tell them I did no
wrong, but my words fell on deaf ears now I
sing my prison song.
I was locked up in the county jail and I started to
dream, when I woke I was still in the cell and
started to scream.
Finally I went before the judge he order I do
three years, I couldn't face my family so I hid
my face and tears.
I wanted to jump up and scream o did no wrong,
but the gavel slammed down now I tell my
prison song.

On a March morning they told me it was time to
go, I felt my life was in slow motion but I didn't
dare say no.
They placed me in the car and I started my trip,
but when I saw my new home I was ready to
flip.

I prayed to God to keep me safe cause I knew I
did no wrong, then the Fulton prison door shut
and birthed my prison song.
As i was placed in a smaller cell, I knew that I
fell into a living hell.
My life would be changed for evermore, I
prayed and wished they would open the door.
But it never did and everyone said I was wrong,
now they read my prison song.

Them on a hot July day I had to repack my
things, and once again be on my way for a new
change.
Not home to my family who love me more than
life, but to a place that held more hate and strife.
So they placed me on a bus to my final stop,
when o reached boonville prison my jaw
dropped.
For I cried on the inside and knew I wasn't
wrong, but things went awry so now I have my
prison song.
From the first to the last day I was scared and it
felt my soul was bared,
I got letters every day and talked to my family
on the phone,I didn't want to feel like an animal
in a cage I wanted to be home. Unfortunately
that was not to be for now everyone knows I
wasn't wrong, they finally listened to my prison
song.

Then it finally happened the guards to me to the
gate, but I wasn't moving to another prison it
was to late.
I did my time and was glad to be going home, no
more waiting for letters or calling on the phone.
I was going to be with the ones I love and
cherish, for what I went through was a test and I
did not perish.
For I knew I wasn't alone when I said I did no
wrong, cause God knew and with his help I
wrote my prison song.

If I died..

If I died tomorrow would you care, the
memories you have would you share?
Would the loss of me passing be to much to bear,
would you talk to me as if I was still there?
Would you visit my grave and tell me what I
missed, would you pray to God and try to make
a wish? If I died tomorrow how would you
remember me, would you remember how I was
or how I wanted to be? Would you still tell me
happy birthday, if you had one chance to talk to
me what so you say? As time moved on would
the memories you have of me fade, or would
they reflect in the choices you made.

Not over yet

We as a family have stood up for one another
through the years,
As we close the doors of our reunion there may
be tears.
But have no fear this is not over yet,
We have generations that we have not met.

As we go into the future we don't know what it
will hold,
as time goes by we will never lose touch and all
stories will be told.
Just cause the doors are closed its not over yet,
As we go through the years a new generation
will emerge I bet.
Just as a passing of the torch the doors will open
once more,
So don't be mad,upset,angry, or sore.

For now it's just time to rest and reflect on the
past,
And remember the family we have cause I know
this isn't the last.
I have faith that once again we as a family will
come together,
So just remember it's not over yet.